Compound Connection Game

Police _____   bow

Flash _____   pack

Bed _____   man

Snow _____   day

Rain _____   cakes

Class _____   plane

Black _____   light

Fire _____   room

Birth _____   ball

Pan _____   boy

Cow _____   room

Air _____   truck

Foot _____   board

Back _____   flake

D1316158

ESL
VOCABULARY
AND
WORD USAGE
Games, Puzzles, and Inventive Exercises

by Imogene Forte
and Mary Ann Pangle

Incentive Publications, Inc.
Nashville, Tennessee

Illustrated by Gayle S. Harvey
Cover by Marta Drayton
Edited by Jean K. Signor

ISBN 0-86530-489-0

2   3   4   5   6   7   8   9   10   08   07   06   05

PRINTED IN THE UNITED STATES OF AMERICA
www.incentivepublications.com

Table of Contents

HOW TO USE THIS BOOK

Student-centered active learning is the focal point of the activities found in ESL Vocabulary and Word Usage Games, Puzzles, and Inventive Exercises, and the content-based nature of the exercises ensures that students are learning more than English. This book will be a valuable tool for all teachers who work with students learning English as a second language (ESL), as well as for teachers working in regular classroom settings.

Each unit is content-based to develop language concepts and strategies connected to a specific vocabulary or word usage skill. Additionally, the exercises in this book offer opportunity for learning, practicing, and mastery of a variety of essential language-based skills. Each exercise includes a list of materials, preparation directions, and player directions. Many exercises have accompanying reproducible activity sheets for immediate classroom skill and/or concept reinforcement. A matrix of essential skills, a skills checklist, a suggested bibliography, and an answer key are also provided. These tools are designed to help teachers plan their lessons and track the achievement of their students. Each activity is for use by ESL students at widely varying levels, while the content base is most appropriate for grades 2–6.

Students need to use learned material, and practice plays an essential role in the mastery and retention of any skill or concept. In addition to individual worksheets, many exercises provide activities that promote cooperative learning and peer tutoring. Cooperative learning activities are essential in an ESL classroom as they enable students to work collaboratively to verbalize, refine, and process newly acquired knowledge and skills. The themes of high-interest on which these activities are based will further encourage student interaction and communication.

This book was written with an eye on the Cognitive Academic Language Learning Approach (CALLA). Accordingly, the exercises encourage the four major conditions of this teaching method: first, to foster a learning environment of high expectations; secondly, to create opportunities to integrate language development with content-based instruction; thirdly, to provide support for teachers in the classroom; and finally, to demonstrate assessment options that empower teachers to plan effective lessons for their students.

The games, puzzles, and exercises within ESL Vocabulary and Word Usage Games, Puzzles, and Inventive Exercises will help teachers make the most effective use of their time in helping their ESL students learn essential vocabulary and word usage skills, improve their use of the English language, and acquire problem-solving skills and concepts important to student success.

Vocabulary and Word Usage Skills Matrix

Content Focus: Vocabulary and Word Usage	Antonyms and Homophones	Speaking	Prefixes and Suffixes	Writing and Spelling	Compound Words	Long and Short Vowels	Following Directions	Learn and Use New Words	Verbs	Count Syllables	Contractions	Root Words
Right Roots												+
Goal Keepers			+					+				
Compound Connection				+	+							
Color Checkers								+				
Caterpillar Capers								+				
ABC Shopping				+				+				
Hidden Treasure							+	+				
Shapes				+			+					
Color Concentration							+	+				
Category Recall			+				+	+				
Body Part Identification				+				+				
Antonym Accuracy	+											
Contraction Castle				+							+	
Phonics Park		+				+						
Syllable Surprise										+		
Action Adventure									+			
Bowling Alley				+			+					
Spinners' Spree				+			+	+				
Magic Manners				+				+				
Let's Write Sentences				+			+	+				
Story Webs				+			+	+				

ESL Vocabulary and Word Usage Games, Puzzles, and Inventive Exercises

Right Roots

Purpose:

Root or Base Words

Materials:

Copies of the activity worksheets

Pencils

Crayons

Number of Players:

One, two, or the entire class

Preparation Directions:

1. Give each player a copy of the activity worksheets and provide students with pencils and crayons.

2. Review root words with the class.

Player Directions:

1. The players read the words on each activity worksheet and write the root words on the plants' roots.

2. The players lightly color the pictures on the activity worksheets.

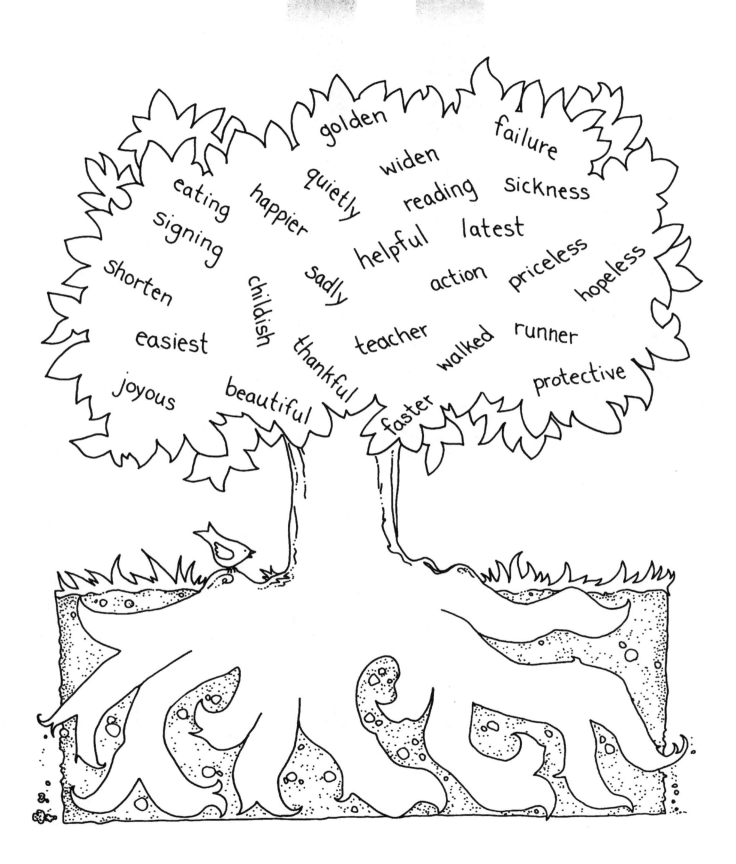

11

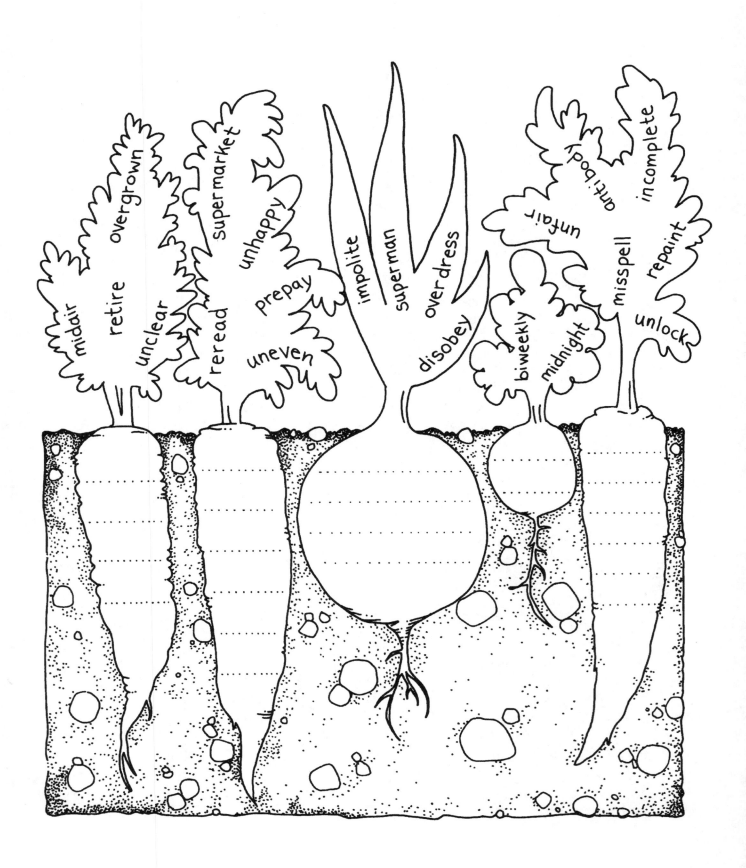

Goal Keepers

Purpose:
Suffixes and Prefixes

Materials:
Game board sheets
Word cards
Materials for game markers

Number of Players:
Two Players

Preparation Directions:
1. Ask each player to draw, color, and cut out a "football" to be used as a marker.
2. Give each group of players a copy of the game board.
3. Cut out the word cards.
4. Review prefixes and suffixes.

Player Directions:
1. The word cards are shuffled and placed face down.
2. The players place a football marker on the opposite ends of the football field game board.
3. The first player draws a card, reads it, and announces whether the word contains a prefix or a suffix.
4. Then the first player states the root word.
5. If the player is correct, he or she moves the football 10 yards.
6. The game continues until one player moves the football 100 yards and scores a goal.

ESL Vocabulary and Word Usage
Games, Puzzles, and Inventive Exercises

reading	prettier	eating
batted	brighter	helpful
wonderful	fastest	started
happily	beautiful	jumped
sweetest	singing	friendly

unbutton	underpaid	disappear
untie	undercover	preschool
relive	disagree	unpaid
uneven	disobey	replant
unequal	disapprove	reopen

15

ESL Vocabulary and Word Usage
Games, Puzzles, and Inventive Exercises

Goal Keepers Game Board

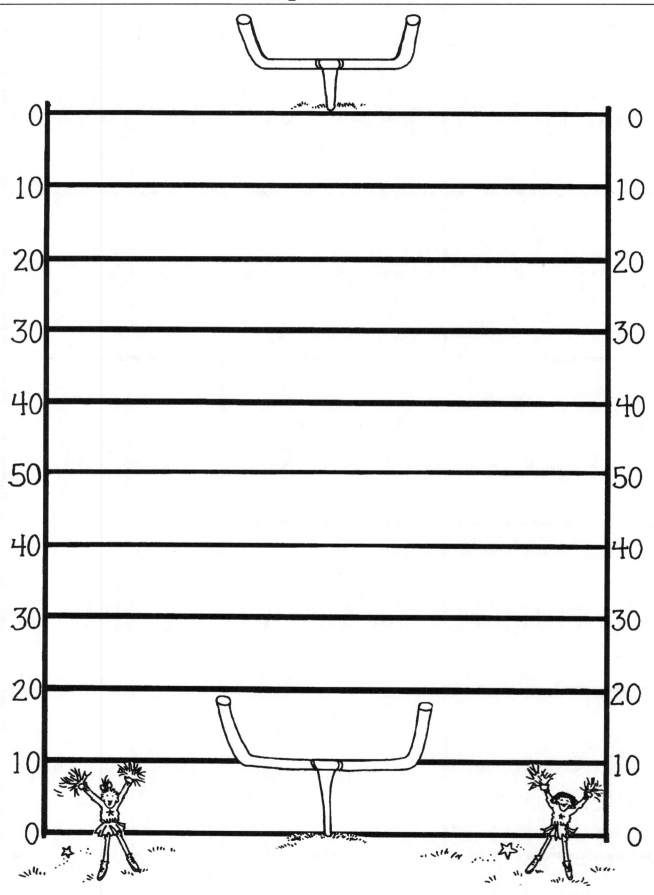

ESL Vocabulary and Word Usage
Games, Puzzles, and Inventive Exercises

16

Compound Connection

Purpose:

    Compound Words

Materials:

    Copy of the game

    Pencils

    Crayons

Number of Players:

    Two

Preparation Directions:

1. Give each player a copy of the game.

2. Give each player a copy of the activity to illustrate compound words.

Player Directions:

1. The game is placed face down before each player.

2. At a given signal, the players turn the game over, read the words in both columns, and write the compound words by selecting words in the right column that match words in the left column.

3. The first player to write all of the compound words wins.

4. The players then illustrate six of the compound words.

Compound Connection Game

Police	_____	bow
Flash	_____	pack
Bed	_____	man
Snow	_____	day
Rain	_____	cakes
Class	_____	plane
Black	_____	light
Fire	_____	room
Birth	_____	ball
Pan	_____	boy
Cow	_____	room
Air	_____	truck
Foot	_____	board
Back	_____	flake

Select one of the compound words to write in each box below. Illustrate each word.

Color Checkers

Purpose:

Recognizing Color Words

Materials:

Copy of the activity

Pencils

Crayons

Number of Players:

One

Preparation Directions:

1. Give each player a copy of the activity worksheet.

2. Provide pencils and crayons.

Player Directions:

1. The player reads the words on the crayon pictures.

2. Then the player circles the color words in the word search.

3. After completing the word search, the player colors the crayon pictures the correct color.

h	o	x	p	u	r	p	l	e	f	y	l	m
y	a	z	e	k	b	i	d	o	t	r	e	d
e	k	v	h	o	w	n	b	l	a	c	k	e
l	b	r	o	w	n	k	f	t	m	g	b	n
l	v	f	w	j	o	r	a	n	g	e	l	g
o	b	a	t	g	r	a	y	v	x	c	u	t
w	h	i	t	e	c	p	u	g	r	e	e	n

ESL Vocabulary and Word Usage
Games, Puzzles, and Inventive Exercises

Caterpillar Capers

Purpose:

Alphabetical Order

Materials:

Copy of caterpillar game board
Copy of ABC's
Scissors
Paste
Crayons

Number of Players:

Two

Preparation Directions:

1. Give each player a copy of the game board and ABC sheets.

2. Provide scissors, paste, and crayons.

Player Directions:

1. The players cut out the ABC cards.

2. The players paste the ABC cards in alphabetical order on the picture of the caterpillar.

3. When completed, the player may color the picture of the caterpillar.

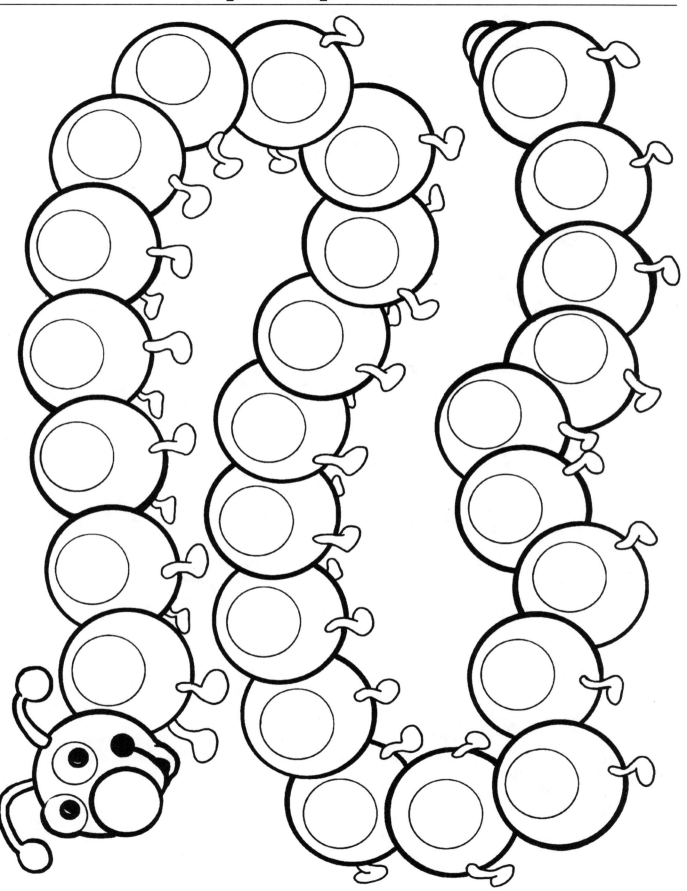

23

ABC Shopping

Purpose:

Alphabetical Order, Vocabulary, Comprehension

Materials:

Copy of game activities
Scissors
Crayons
Paste

Number of Players:

One, two, or the entire class

Preparation Directions:

1. Give each player a copy of the game activities and provide scissors, pencils, paste, and crayons.

2. Review alphabetical order.

Player Directions:

1. The players cut out the word cards.

2. The players pretend that they are shopping in a grocery store.

3. The word cards are pasted on the grocery shelves in alphabetical order.

4. Then the players draw and color a picture that represents each word that has been pasted on the grocery shelves.

| Ketchup | Raisins | Grapes | Yogurt | Flour |

| Pineapple | Eggs | Milk | Tea | Bananas |

| Soap | Lemons | Hamburger | Water | Jam |

| Dog food | Quart of juice | Cereal | Oranges |

| Vegetables | Ice cream |

Apples

Hidden Treasure

Purpose:
    Vocabulary Development

Materials:
    Copy of Maze
    Copy of Puzzle
    Pencils
    Answers to
        Treasure Words Puzzle:
            1. elephant
            2. butterfly
            3. monkey
            4. giraffe
            5. chicken
            6. snake
            7. tiger
            8. camel
            9. rabbit

Number of Players:
    One, two, or the entire class

Preparation Directions:
    1. Give each player a copy of the maze and puzzle sheets.
    2. Provide pencils.

Player Directions:
    1. The players follow the path through the maze to reach the treasure chest.
    2. There is a puzzle "inside" the treasure chest.
    3. Students subtract and add letters to make words to complete the puzzle.
    4. The players may illustrate the words on the back of the puzzle.

Hidden Treasure Maze

ESL Vocabulary and Word Usage
Games, Puzzles, and Inventive Exercises

Hidden Treasure Puzzle

1. eap – ap + lid – id + epy – y + hok – ok + at – t + nt
2. abc – ac + wux – wx + ott – o + gef – gf + orf – o + mlk – mk + iay – ia
3. men – en + omt – mt + not – ot + kh – h + ey
4. get – et + ice – ce + rae – e + foot – oot + of – o + egg – gg
5. abc – ab + hat – at + kid – kd + cat – at + mok – mo + few – fw + not – ot
6. pls – pl + and – ad + qau – qu + kav – av + red – rd
7. cat – ca + aei – ae + got – ot + wek – wk + rat – at
8. act – at + age – ge + mom – om + yes – ys + let – et
9. wor – wo + add – dd + sbu – su + boy – oy + ing – ng + hot – ho

1. _____

2. _____

3. _____

4. _____

5. _____

6. _____

7. _____

8. _____

9. _____

Shapes

Purpose:
  Vocabulary comprehension

Materials:
  Copy of activity worksheets
  Scissors
  Crayons

Number of Players:
  One, two, or the entire class.

Preparation Directions:

1. Give each player a copy of the activity worksheets and provide scissors and crayons.

2. Review shapes.

Player Directions:

1. Each player cuts out the shapes and matches and pastes the shape with the matching vocabulary word.

2. The players follow the directions on the activity worksheets, cut out the different sized shapes, and use the shapes to create a picture .

3. They then use crayons, to color the picture they created.

4. Then, the players share and discuss their pictures.

Shapes Game Cards

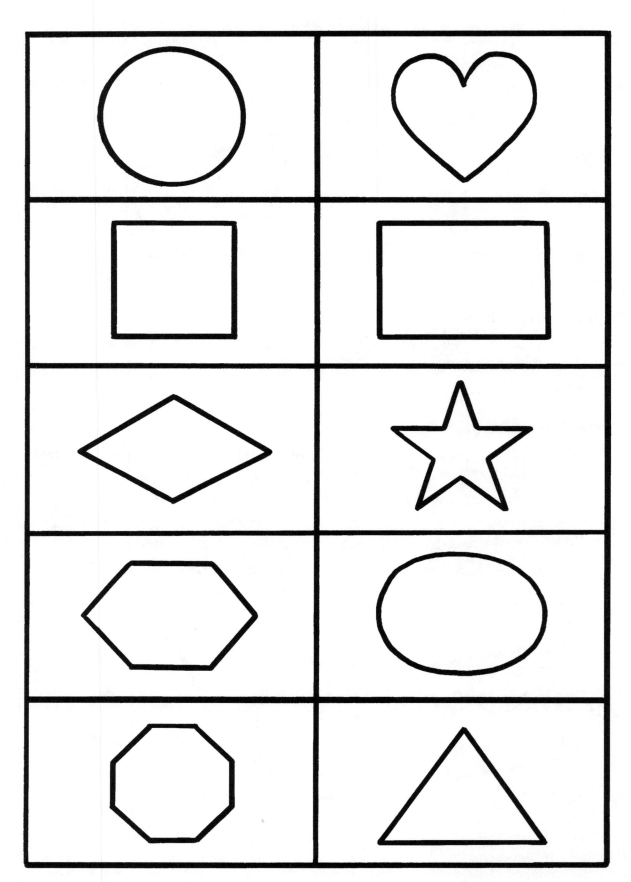

Shapes Activity

Paste the correct shape in the box with its name.

Octagon		Hexagon	
Rectangle		Oval	
Square		Heart	
Diamond		Star	
Circle		Triangle	

ESL Vocabulary and Word Usage
Games, Puzzles, and Inventive Exercises

Shapes Activity Follow-Up

Cut out the shapes. Make a picture using all of the shapes.
Paste the picture on another piece of paper.
Color the picture.

Color Concentration

Purpose:
Vocabulary - Comprehension

Materials:
Copy of game cards
Scissors
Crayons

Number of Players:
Two

Preparation Directions:
1. Each group of players cuts out the game cards.
2. One card is colored to match each of the color words.

Player Directions:
1. The game cards are shuffled and placed face down.
2. The first player draws two cards.
3. If the cards match, one color word and one color card, the player keeps the two cards.
4. If the cards do not match, the player places them back down on the table and tries to remember where they are.
5. The players take turns drawing cards until all cards are matched.
6. The player with the most cards wins the game.

ESL Vocabulary and Word Usage
Games, Puzzles, and Inventive Exercises

Color Concentration Game Cards

color blue ↓ | color green ↓

| blue | | green | |

color red ↓ | color orange ↓

| red | | orange | |

color yellow ↓ | color black ↓

| yellow | | black | |

color purple ↓ | color pink ↓

| purple | | pink | |

color brown ↓ | color gray ↓

| brown | | gray | |

ESL Vocabulary and Word Usage Games, Puzzles, and Inventive Exercises

Body Part and Clothing Identification

Purpose:

Vocabulary

Materials:

Copy of game activities

Pencils

Crayons

Number of Players:

The entire class

Preparation Directions:

1. Give each player a copy of the activity worksheets and provide students with pencils and crayons.

2. Review body parts and clothing.

Player Directions:

1. The players take the activity worksheets and place them face down.

2. At a given signal, the worksheets are turned over and the players write the names of the body parts and clothing in the correct spaces.

3. The first player to complete the activities wins the game.

Body Part Identification Game — Boy

ESL Vocabulary and Word Usage
Games, Puzzles, and Inventive Exercises

Clothing Identification Game — Girl

*ESL Vocabulary and Word Usage
Games, Puzzles, and Inventive Exercises*

Category Recall

Purpose:

Vocabulary

Materials:

Activity Worksheets
Pencils
Crayons

Number of Players:

One, two, or the entire class

Preparation Directions:

1. Give each player a copy of the activity worksheets.

2. Provide pencils and crayons for the students.

Player Directions:

1. The players may work in small cooperative groups.

2. The players write four words that are related to each category.

3. Then the players illustrate one of the words in each category.

Category Recall Game Activity

Directions: Write four words that fit each category.
Then illustrate one word in each box.

Family	Sports	Clothes	Weather
_____	_____	_____	_____
_____	_____	_____	_____
_____	_____	_____	_____
_____	_____	_____	_____

Transportation	Furniture	Holidays	Foods
_____	_____	_____	_____
_____	_____	_____	_____
_____	_____	_____	_____
_____	_____	_____	_____

41

ESL Vocabulary and Word Usage
Games, Puzzles, and Inventive Exercises

Category Recall Game Activity Cont.

Directions: Write four words that fit each category.
Then illustrate one word in each box.

Months	Days	Classes	Feelings
_____	_____	_____	_____
_____	_____	_____	_____
_____	_____	_____	_____
_____	_____	_____	_____

Signs	Body Parts	School Supplies	Jobs
_____	_____	_____	_____
_____	_____	_____	_____
_____	_____	_____	_____
_____	_____	_____	_____

Category Recall Game Activity Cont.

Directions: Write four words that fit each category.
Then illustrate one word in each box.

Animals	Toys	Colors	Shapes
_____	_____	_____	_____
_____	_____	_____	_____
_____	_____	_____	_____
_____	_____	_____	_____

Buildings	Countries	Books	Stores
_____	_____	_____	_____
_____	_____	_____	_____
_____	_____	_____	_____
_____	_____	_____	_____

ESL Vocabulary and Word Usage
Games, Puzzles, and Inventive Exercises

Antonym Accuracy

Purpose:

Antonyms

Materials:

Copy of game board
Pencils

Number of Players:

Two or the entire class

Preparation Directions:

1. Give a copy of the game board to each player.

2. Provide pencils for each player.

3. Review antonyms with the class.

Player Directions:

1. Each player begins at "START," and reads the word in the first space.
   Then, the player writes its antonym on the line below the word.

2. The game continues until each player reaches "FINISH."

Antonym Accuracy Game Board

START

large	sad	open	man	new	wet
___	___	___	___	___	___
cold	bad	below	stop	fast	old
___	___	___	___	___	___
dirty	sick	father	run	sunny	pull
___	___	___	___	___	___
asleep	sweet	girl	enter	yes	pretty
___	___	___	___	___	___
empty	always	night	easy	front	loud
___	___	___	___	___	___
under	stand	round	night	smile	dark
___	___	___	___	___	___

FINISH!

*ESL Vocabulary and Word Usage
Games, Puzzles, and Inventive Exercises*

Happy Homophones

Purpose:

   Vocabulary - Homophones

Materials:

   Copy of the game
   Pencils
   Crayons

Number of Players:

   Two

Preparation Directions:

   1. Give each player a copy of the game.

   2. Provide pencils and crayons.

   3. Review homophones: homophones are words that sound alike, but have different spellings and meanings.

Player Directions:

   1. The players place the game face down on the desk.

   2. At a given signal, the players turn the game over and write a homophone in each balloon shape.

   3. The first player to complete the game correctly wins the game.

   4. The balloons may be colored and decorated.

Happy Homophones Activity

Write a homophone for each word in the balloons below.

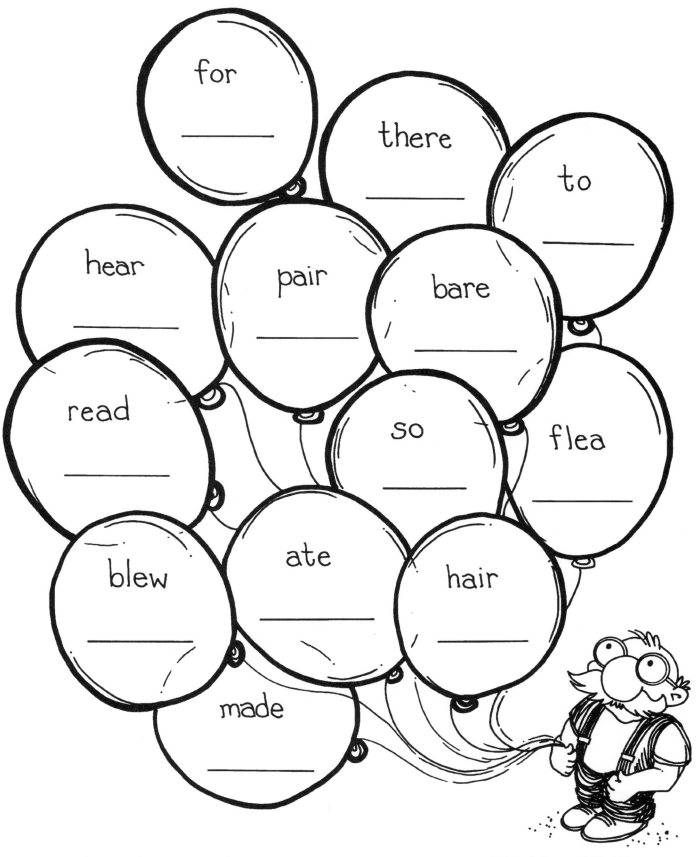

for _____

there _____

to _____

hear _____

pair _____

bare _____

read _____

so _____

flea _____

blew _____

ate _____

hair _____

made _____

*ESL Vocabulary and Word Usage
Games, Puzzles, and Inventive Exercises*

All About Adjectives

Purpose:

Vocabulary

Materials:

Copy of adjective games
Pencils

Number of Players:

Two

Preparation Directions:

1. Give each player a copy of the adjective worksheet.

2. Provide pencils to the students.

3. Review adjectives with the entire class.

Player Directions:

1. The players take the All About Adjectives Mountain worksheet and place it face down.

2. At a given signal, the players climb up and down the mountain by writing a noun for each adjective.

3. The players must use a different noun each time.

4. The player who completes the game first, wins.

5. Using the All About Adjectives Suitcase worksheet, players write a different adjective for each object that is in the suitcase.

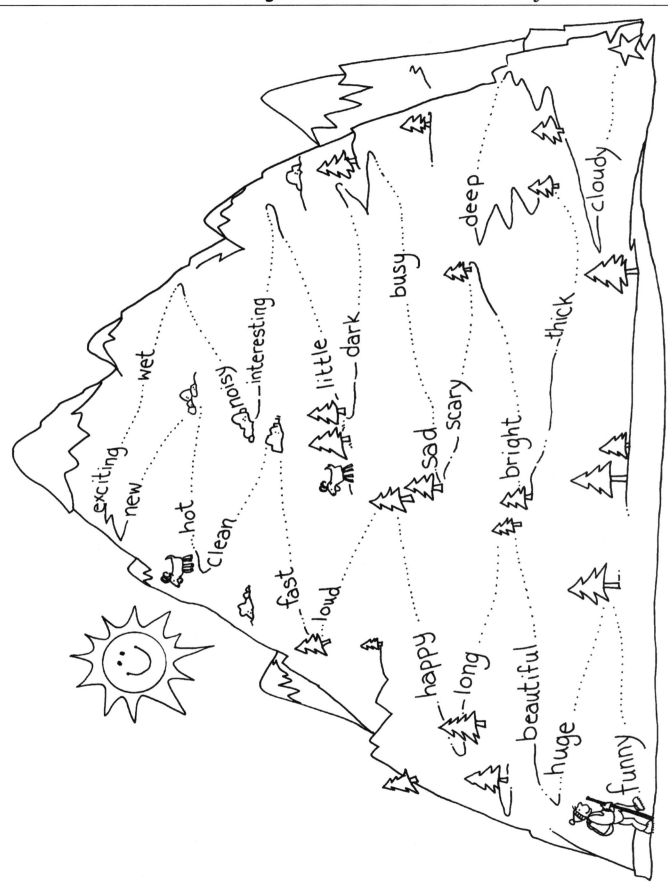

All About Adjectives Suitcase Activity

Directions: Pretend that you are going on a trip. Write an adjective for each object in the suitcase.

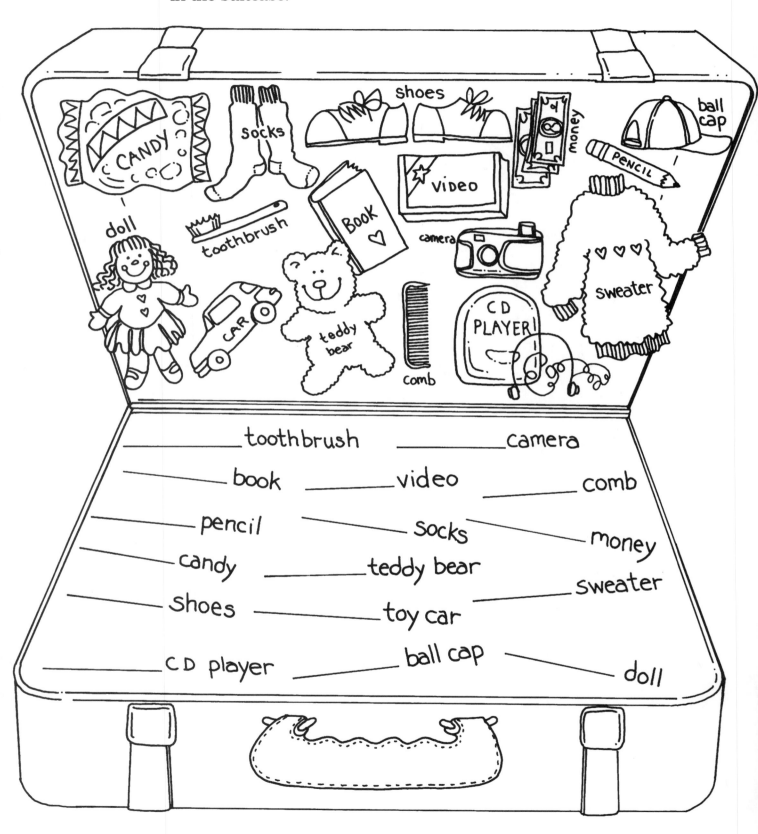

_____ toothbrush   _____ camera

_____ book   _____ video   _____ comb

_____ pencil   _____ socks   _____ money

_____ candy   _____ teddy bear   _____ sweater

_____ shoes   _____ toy car

_____ CD player   _____ ball cap   _____ doll

Contraction Castle

Purpose:

Contractions

Materials:

Copy of the game

Copy of the sentence activity worksheet

Pencils

Crayons or colored pencils

Number of Players:

One, two, or the entire class.

Preparation Directions:

1. Give each player a copy of the game.

2. When the game is completed, give each player a sentence activity worksheet.

Player Directions:

1. The players pretend to tour a "Contraction Castle."

2. As the players "walk" through the castle, they will see many words.

3. The players write a contraction under each group of words.

4. When the "Contraction Castle" tour is completed, players may use crayons or colored pencils to lightly color the castle.

5. They then write ten sentences using one contraction in each sentence.

*ESL Vocabulary and Word Usage
Games, Puzzles, and Inventive Exercises*

Contraction Castle Game

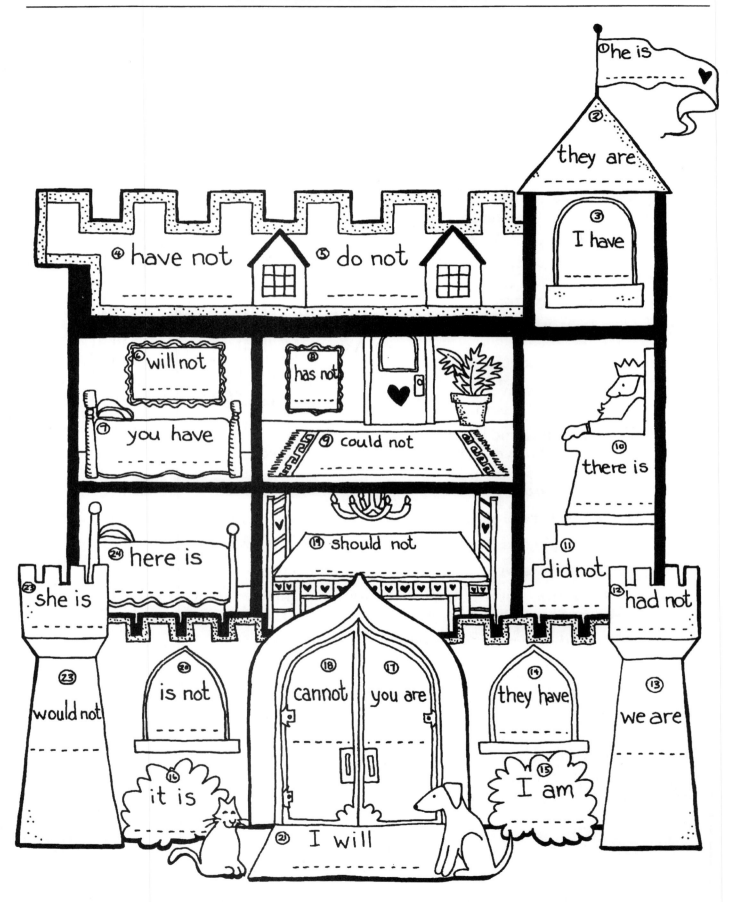

1. he is
2. they are
3. I have
4. have not
5. do not
6. will not
7. you have
8. has not
9. could not
10. there is
11. did not
12. had not
13. we are
14. they have
15. I am
16. it is
17. you are
18. cannot
19. should not
20. is not
21. I will
22. here is
23. would not
24. she is

Contraction Castle Game Cont.

Choose ten contractions and write a sentence using each one.

1. _____

2. _____

3. _____

4. _____

5. _____

6. _____

7. _____

8. _____

9. _____

10. _____

Phonics Park

Purpose:

Long and Short Vowels

Materials:

Copy of the game

Pencils

Crayons

Number of Players:

Two

Preparation Directions:

1. Give each player a copy of the game, and provide students with pencils and crayons.

2. Review long and short vowels with the entire class.

Player Directions:

1. The player takes the game board and places it face down.

2. At a given signal, the players turn the game board over and begin the game.

3. The players read the word above each picture.

4. If the vowel sound in the word is long, the players write four words with a long vowel sound.

5. If the vowel sound in the word is short, the players write four words with a short vowel sound.

6. The first player to complete the activity wins the game.

7. The players may then color the park scene.

Phonics Park Game

*ESL Vocabulary and Word Usage
Games, Puzzles, and Inventive Exercises*

Syllable Surprise

Purpose:

Spelling - Syllables

Materials:

Copy of the game board
Two copies of the blank cards
Scissors
Spelling words
Pencils
Markers for the game

Number of Players:

Two

Preparation Directions:

1. Give each group of two players a copy of the game board.

2. Cut out the game cards.

3. Write one spelling word on each game card.

Player Directions:

1. The game cards are shuffled and placed face down.

2. The players place the markers on "Start" on the game board.

3. The first player draws a card, pronounces the word, and moves one space for each syllable in the word.

4. If the answer is incorrect, he or she moves back one space.

5. The game continues until one player reaches "Finish" and wins the game.

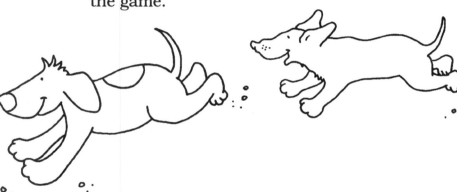

Syllable Surprise Blank Game Cards

ESL Vocabulary and Word Usage
Games, Puzzles, and Inventive Exercises

Syllable Surprise Game Board

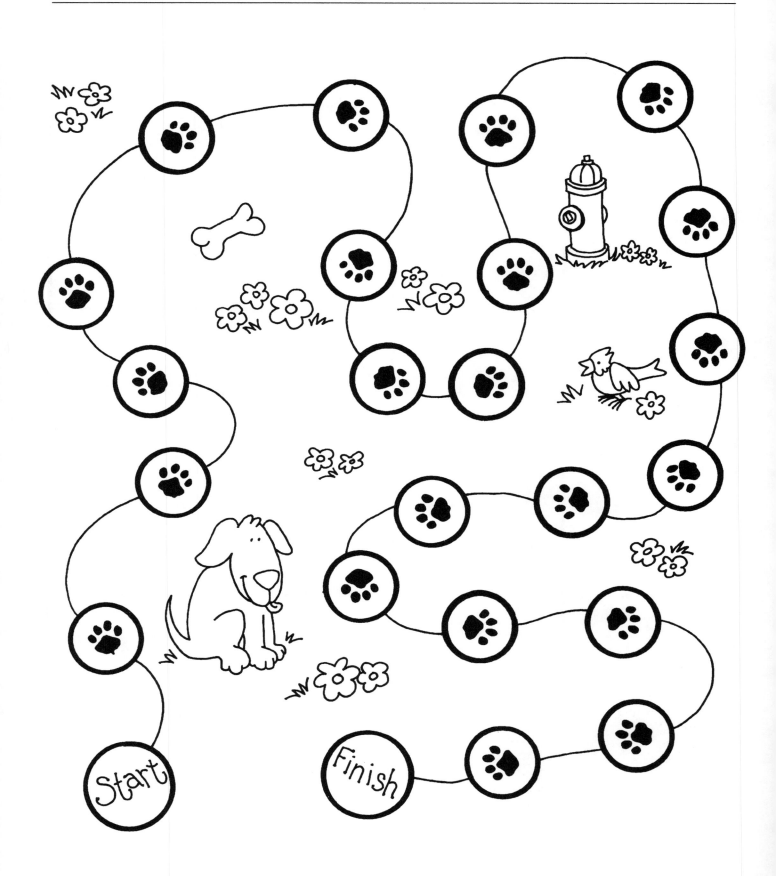

ESL Vocabulary and Word Usage
Games, Puzzles, and Inventive Exercises

58

Action Adventure

Purpose:

Verbs

Materials:

Copy of the Word Search
Pencils

Number of Players:

One or the entire class.

Preparation Directions:

1. Review verbs that are action words.

2. Give each player a copy of the Word Search.

Player Directions:

1. The players circle the action words in the Word Search.

2. The players may work individually or in small groups.

ESL Vocabulary and Word Usage
Games, Puzzles, and Inventive Exercises

Action Adventure Word Search

Find and circle all of the action verbs listed.

drink
draw
sleep
sing
write
run
eat
work
sit
jump
stand
push
pull
call
talk
kick
walk
ring
open
play
look
speak
read
buy
fly

w	o	r	k	x	p	j	u	m	p	s	i	t
a	a	u	i	t	u	b	p	q	u	t	c	d
l	k	n	c	a	l	l	e	n	s	a	e	r
k	s	b	k	l	l	z	a	t	h	n	o	i
r	i	n	g	k	b	s	t	d	h	d	n	n
m	n	o	w	r	w	l	w	o	p	e	n	k
w	g	t	i	e	r	e	h	m	d	r	a	w
l	o	o	k	a	i	e	s	p	e	a	k	j
r	e	d	s	d	t	p	l	a	y	c	a	r
b	u	y	a	n	e	t	h	e	y	f	l	y

Bowling Alley

Purpose:

Spelling

Materials:

Cardboard

Felt tip pens

Scissors

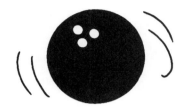

Number of Players:

Two

Preparation Directions:

1. Make bowling pins from cardboard and number each pin.

2. On the back of each pin write a spelling word. The higher the number of pins, the more difficult the word.

Player Directions:

1. Set up the two sets of pins.

2. One player calls the number of a pin. The opponent reads the word on the back. If the player spells it correctly, he has knocked over a pin.

3. Players take turns choosing pins and spelling. The more difficult words are on the pins with the highest numbers.

4. The first player to knock over all the pins wins the game.

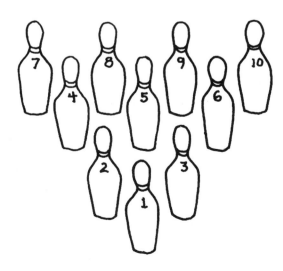
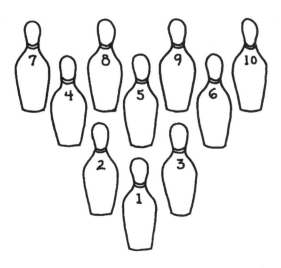

Bowling Alley

Spinners' Spree

Purpose:

Spelling

Materials:

Tag board

Felt tip pens

Scissors

Paper fastener

Number of Players:

Two to four

Preparation Directions:

1. Cut a circle and an arrow from the tag board. Fasten the arrow in the middle with a brass paper fastener.

2. Write spelling words appropriate to individual student ability levels on the circle.

Player Directions:

1. One player spins the dial to find a word for another player to spell.

2. The game continues until all the players have had a chance to spell all the words.

3. Award one point for each correctly spelled word. The player with the most points wins the game.

Spinners' Spree

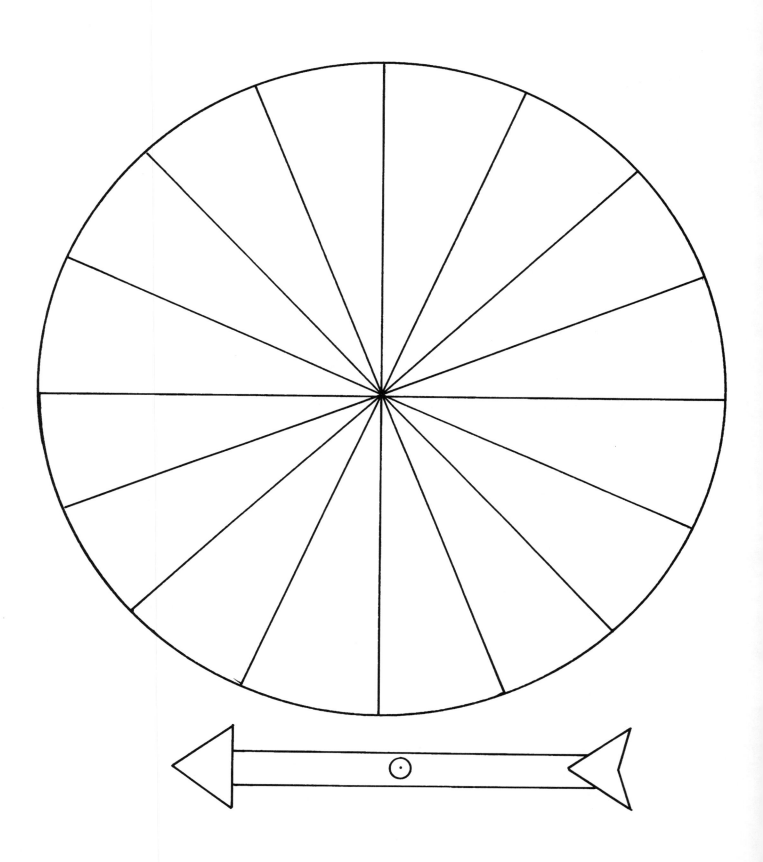

Magic Manners

Purpose:

Choose correct words in writing.

Materials:

Copy of the game board
Scissors
Game cards
Markers

Number of Players:

Two

Preparation Directions:

1. Give the players one copy of the game board and one copy of the game cards.

2. Provide scissors and markers.

3. Review manners with the class.

Player Directions:

1. The players cut out the game cards and place them face down.

2. The players place the markers on "Start."

3. The first player draws a card, reads it, and gives the answer according to nice manners.

4. If the answer is correct, the player moves one space.

5. The game continues until one player reaches "Finish" and wins the game.

Someone gives you a gift.	You meet a new friend.	It is your friend's birthday.	You want to borrow a pencil.
The teacher gives you a fun activity.	You are served something you don't like.	A friend invited you to a party.	You answer the telephone.
You accidentally make a classmate drop her books.	You come into the classroom late.	You ask your parents for money.	You leave a friend's house after a party.
A classmate speaks badly about another classmate.	A friend wins a special race in P.E..	Two adults are talking and you need to speak with one of them.	Introduce your parents to your teacher.
Lose one turn.	Take another turn.		

Magic Manners Game Board

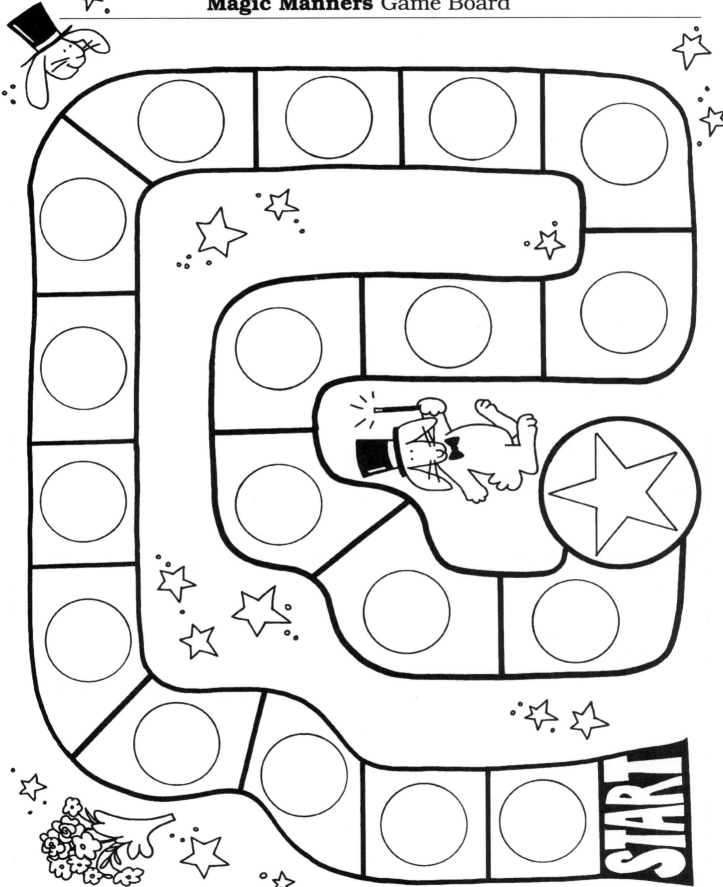

ESL Vocabulary and Word Usage
Games, Puzzles, and Inventive Exercises

Let's Write Sentences

Purpose:

Writing sentences

Materials:

Game Worksheets
Pencils
Crayons

Number of Players:

Two

Preparation Directions:

1. Distribute the game worksheets and provide pencils and crayons.

2. Review writing complete sentences.

Player Directions:

1. This is a cooperative group game.

2. The players work together using the words on the worksheets to make complete sentences.

3. When the game has been completed, students may lightly color the pictures.

Let's Write Sentences Activity

See how many sentences you can write using these words:

elephant	the	gray	circus	has	trunk
a	ears	is	long	big	in

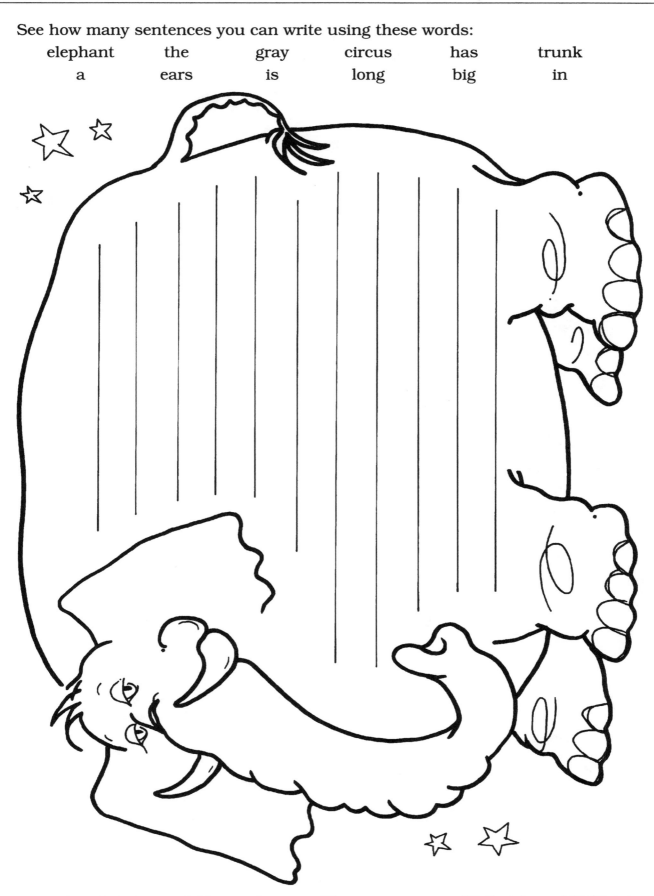

*ESL Vocabulary and Word Usage
Games, Puzzles, and Inventive Exercises*

Let's Write Sentences Activity

See how many sentences you can write using these words:

monkey	the	me	in	tree
I	laugh	zoo	brown	
like	funny	makes		
lives	a			
is				

Let's Write Sentences Activity

See how many sentences you can write using these words:

bus	the	boys
it	yellow	girls
to	and	is
ride	school	fun

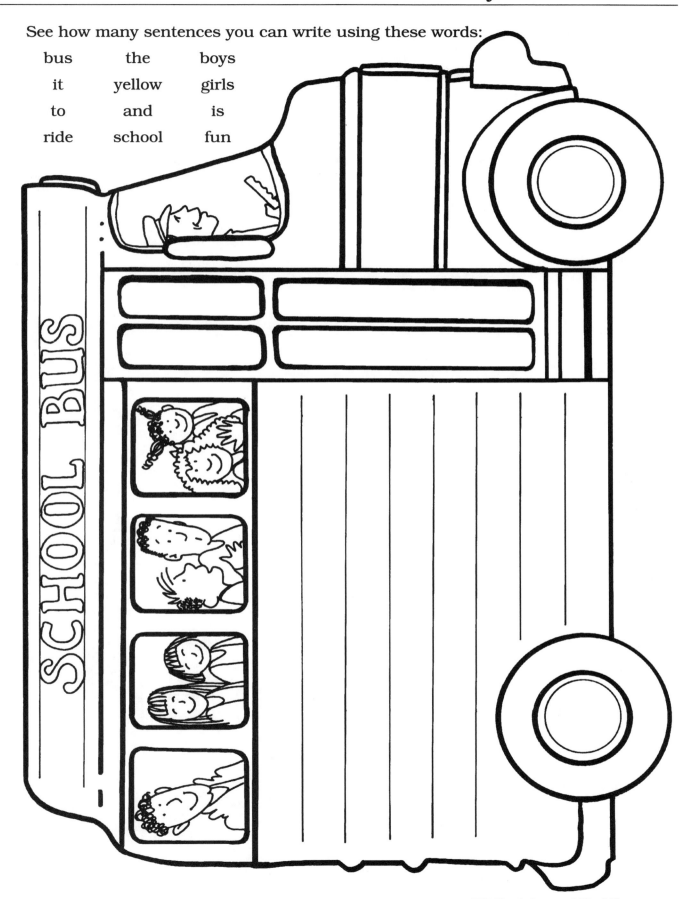

ESL Vocabulary and Word Usage
Games, Puzzles, and Inventive Exercises

Let's Write Sentences Activity

See how many sentences you can write using these words:

school	go	read	friends	I	at
write	teacher	to	play	have	my
eat	nice	is	like	fun	the

PUBLIC SCHOOL

Story Webs

Purpose:
Writing

Materials:
Activity Worksheets
Pencils
Dictionaries

Number of Players:
One or the entire class.

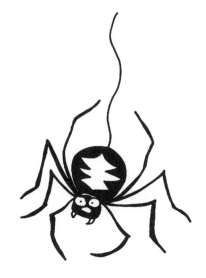

Preparation Directions:
1. Distribute activity worksheets and provide students with pencils and dictionaries.
2. Review steps in writing a story from a story web.

Player Directions:
1. The players create a story by writing one or two sentences about each word that is written on the web.
2. The players and the teacher have a conference to edit the story.
3. After editing the story, the players rewrite the story.
4. The players will enjoy sharing their stories.

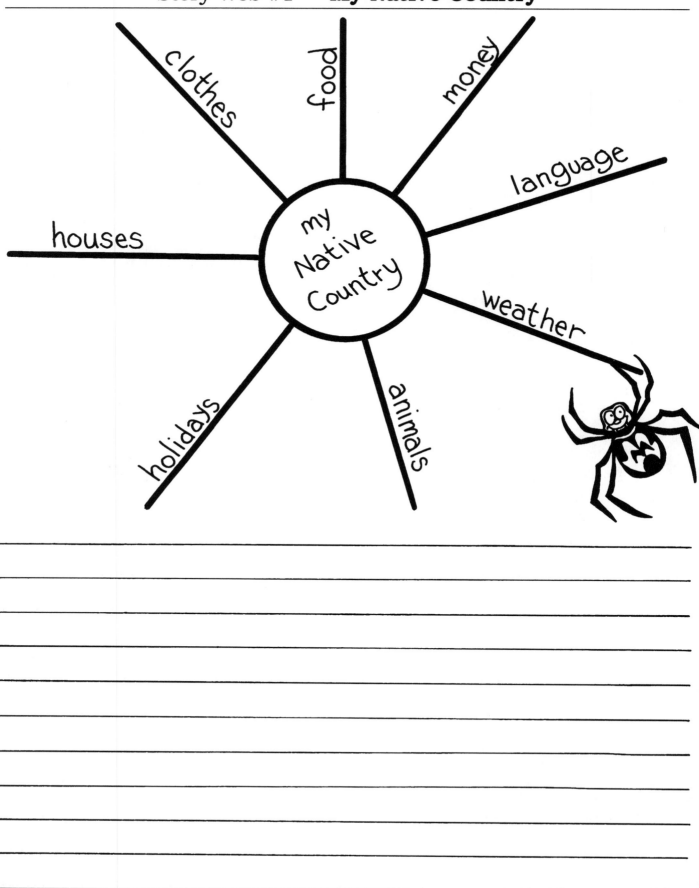

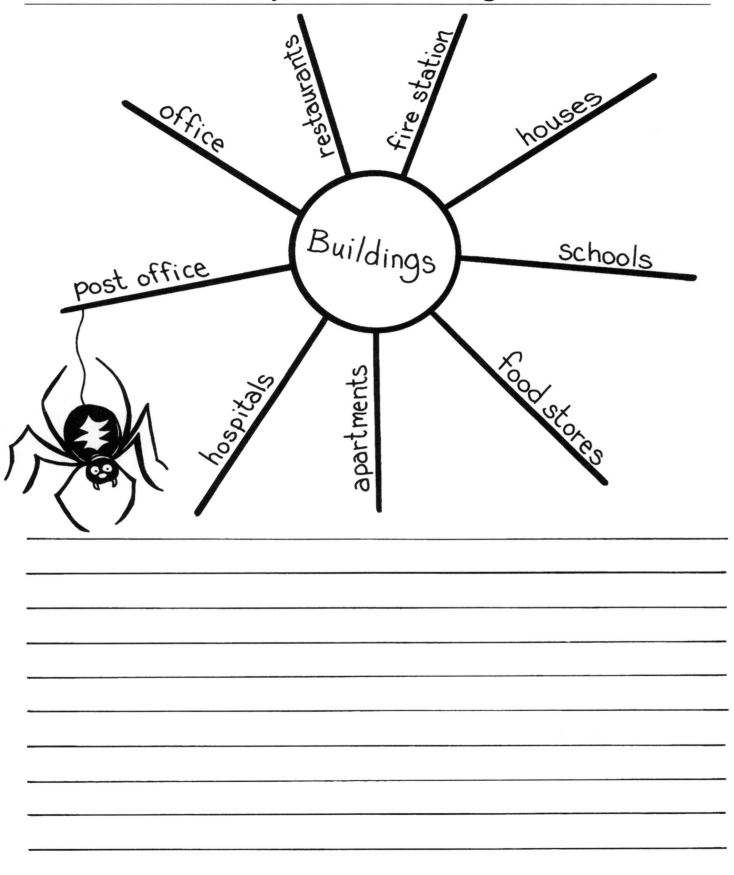

75

Annotated Bibliography
for the ESL Teacher

BASIC/Not Boring Reading Comprehension, Grades 4-5. Imogene Forte and Marjorie Frank. Nashville, Incentive Publications, Inc., 1998
Imaginative activities covering essential reading skills such as: main ideas, finding information, sequencing, and paraphrasing.

BASIC/Not Boring Spelling, Grades 4-5, Imogene Forte and Marjorie Frank. Nashville, Incentive Publications, Inc., 1999
Imaginative activities covering essential spelling skills such as: identifying correctly spelled and misspelled words, learning the "ie" rules, and distinguishing among homophones.

BASIC/Not Boring Reading, Grades 2-3. Imogene Forte and Marjorie Frank. Nashville, Incentive Publications, Inc., 1998
Imaginative activities covering essential reading skills such as: main idea, sequencing, charts, directions, and characters.

BASIC/Not Boring Spelling, Grades 2-3. Imogene Forte and Marjorie Frank. Nashville, Incentive Publications, Inc. 2000
Imaginative activities covering essential spelling skills such as: compound words, consonant blends, and frequently misspelled words.

The Cooperative Learning Guide and Planning Pak for the Primary Grades. Imogene Forte and Joy MacKenzie. Nashville, Incentive Publications, Inc., 1992
Includes an overview of cooperative learning and thematic teaching, content mini-units, interdisciplinary units, and thematic learning stations.

Cooperative Learning Teacher Timesavers. Imogene Forte. Nashville, Incentive Publications, Inc., 1992
Contains summaries, warm-ups, bulletin boards, and cooperative activities, and motivational ideas, as well as ready-to-use reproducible aids, badges, clip art, reports, worksheets, and records.

Creating Connection: Learning to Appreciate Diversity. Dorothy Michener. Nashville, Incentive Publications, Inc., 1995
Provides practical strategies and workable solutions for educators striving to help their students recognize, understand, and appreciate diversity.

Easy Art Projects to Teach Global Awareness. Lynn Brisson. Nashville, Incentive Publications, Inc., 1993
Topics covered include map skills, the 50 United States, the 7 continents, desert and ocean study, and more!

ESL Active Learning Lessons: 15 Complete Content-Based Units to Reinforce Language Skills and Concepts. Imogene Forte and Mary Ann Pangle. Nashville, Incentive Publications, Inc., 2001
Provides practice and reinforcement in the use of listening, speaking, reading and writing.

ESL Content-Based Language Games, Puzzles, and Inventive Exercises. Imogene Forte and Mary Ann Pangle. Nashville, Incentive Publications, Inc., 2001
Offers useable guides to learn, practice, and master a variety of language-based skills, focusing on math, social studies, and science.

ESL Reading and Spelling Games, Puzzles, and Inventive Exercises. Imogene Forte and Mary Ann Pangle. Nashville, Incentive Publications, Inc., 2001
Offers useable guides to learn, practice, and master a variety of language-based skills, focusing on reading and spelling.

Hands-On Math. Kathleen Fletcher. Nashville, Incentive Publications, Inc., 1996
Contains all the essentials and extras for teaching number-sense concepts. Included ideas for using stamps, stickers, beans, rice, tiles, and number lines and manipulatives in the classroom.

Internet Quest. Catherine Halloran Cook and Janet McGivney Pfeifer. Nashville, Incentive Publications, Inc., 2000
Designed to engage students in learning on the web. 101 new sites to explore covering exciting topics such as: art and music, geography and travel, nature and science.

Language Arts Folder Fun. Kathy Blankenhorn and Joanne Richards. Nashville, Incentive Publications, Inc., 1995
Folder games target and reinforce the fundamentals of language arts.

Learning to Learn: Strengthening Study Skills and Brain Power. Gloria Frender. Nashville, Incentive Publications, Inc., 1990
Includes step-by-step procedures for improving organizational skills, time management, problem solving, power reading, test taking, memory skills, and more!

Multicultural Plays: A Many-Splendored Tapestry Honoring Our Global Community. Judy Mecca. Nashville, Incentive Publications, Inc., 1999
Easily-produced plays allow students to learn about and develop respect for different cultures. A brief cultural lesson accompanies each play to ensure an authentic performance.

On the Loose With Dr. Seuss. Shirley Cook. Nashville, Incentive Publications, Inc., 1994
Each literature-based unit includes background information about Dr. Seuss and one of his stories, extended thinking and writing exercises, and special imaginative activities.

Reading Reinforcers for the Primary Grades. Imogene Forte. Nashville, Incentive Publications, Inc., 1994
A collection of teacher-directed interactive projects, creative worksheets, and independent and group activities.

Seasonal Activities for Classroom Creativity. Kitty Hazler. Nashville, Incentive Publications, Inc., 1999
High-interest lessons to nurture creativity and promote higher order thinking skills within a seasonal theme. Students gain fluency and originality.

Using Literature to Learn About Children Around the World. Judith Cochran. Nashville, Incentive Publications, Inc., 1993
Lesson plans outline specific activities to develop social and global awareness and to strengthen vocabulary and thinking skills.

Answer Key

Page 11

The correct root words
   are as follows:

   beauty, protect, hope, fail,
   easy, thank, price, sad,
   sign, happy, help, read,
   gold, sick, late, walk, joy,
   short, act, fast, child, eat,
   run, wide, quiet, teach

Page 12

The correct root words
   are as follows:

   air, grow, tire, clear,
   market, read, happy, pay,
   even, polite, man, dress,
   obey, week, night, fair,
   body, paint, spell,
   complete, lock

Pages 14–15

Words with suffixes:	Words with prefixes:
Reading	Unbutton
Batted	Untie
Wonderful	Relive
Happily	Uneven
Sweetest	Unequal
Prettier	Underpaid
Brighter	Undercover
Fastest	Disagree
Beautiful	Disobey
Singing	Disapprove
Eating	Disappear
Helpful	Preschool
Started	Unpaid
Jumped	Replant
Friendly	Reopen

Page 18

Policeman	Fire truck
Flashlight	Birthday
Bedroom	Pancakes
Snowflake	Cowboy
Rainbow	Airplane
Classroom	Football
Blackboard	Backpack

Page 21

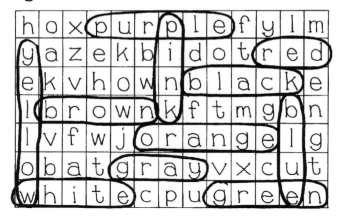

Page 30

1. elephant
2. butterfly
3. monkey
4. giraffe
5. chicken
6. snake
7. tiger
8. camel
9. rabbit

Page 45

Antonyms:

   Large – small
   Sad – happy
   Open – closed
   Man – woman
   New – old
   Wet – dry
   Cold – hot
   Bad – good
   Below – above
   Stop – go
   Fast – slow
   Old – new
   Dirty – clean
   Sick – healthy
   Father – mother

Run – walk
Sunny – cloudy
Pull – push
Asleep – awake
Sweet – sour
Girl – boy
Enter – exit
Yes – No
Pretty – ugly
Empty – full
Always – never
Night – day
Easy – difficult
Front – rear
Load – unload
Under – over
Stand – sit
Round – concave
Night – day
Smile – frown
Dark – light

Page 47

Homophones
For – four
There – their, they're
Hear – here
Pair – pear
To – two, too
Bare – bear
So – sew
Read – reed
Ate – eight
Blew – blue
Made – maid
Hair – heir
Flea – flee

Page 52

He is – he's
They are – they're
I have – I've
Do not – don't
Have not – haven't
Will not – won't
You have – you've
Could not – couldn't
I am – I'm
It is – It's
You are – you're
Cannot – can't
It is – It's
They have – They've
Has not – hasn't
There is – there's
Did not – didn't
Had not – hadn't
We are – we're
Here is – here's
Would not – wouldn't
She is – she's
I will – I'll
Is not – Isn't

Page 60

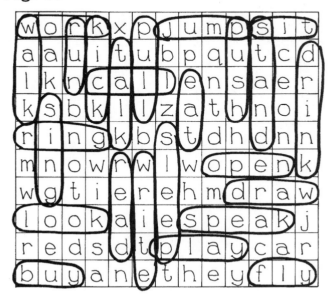

Copyright ©2001 by Incentive Publications, Inc.
Nashville, TN.

79

*ESL Vocabulary and Word Usage
Games, Puzzles, and Inventive Exercises*